Read Me First

- All information supplied in this guide is for educational purpose only and users bear the responsibility for using it.

- Although I took tremendous effort to ensure that all information provided in this guide are correct, I will welcome your suggestions if you find out that any information provided in this guide is inadequate or you find a better way of doing some of the actions mentioned in this guide. All correspondence should be sent to pharmibrahimguides@gmail.com

About This Guide

This is a very thorough, no-nonsense guide, useful for both experts and newbies.

This is a very detailed and extensive guide about **Microsoft Edge, Cortana, and Mail app on Microsoft Surface Pro 4 and Microsoft Surface Book**. It is full of actionable steps, hints, notes, screenshots and suggestions.

This guide is particularly useful for newbies and seniors; nevertheless I strongly believe that even the techy guys will find benefits reading it.

Enjoy yourself as you go through this very comprehensive guide.

How to Use this Guide

This guide is packed with a lot of information and I will like that you use it as a reference guide.

When I say you should press any key combination, for example when I say you should press **Ctrl + J** or just any other key, what I mean is that you should press and hold keyboard's Control (**Ctrl**) and then press **J** key. You can also press these two keys simultaneously if you can.

Lastly, I have based most of the information contained in this guide on the assumption that you are going to be controlling your Microsoft Surface Pro 4/Microsoft Surface Book with the trackpad. However, you will still get similar result by using your finger or Surface pen to control the touchscreen. For example, when I tell you to click an item using the trackpad, you will get a similar result if you tap the item with a finger or Surface pen.

Table of Contents

Microsoft Edge

Introduction

Gone are the days of Internet Explorer(IE); the advent of Microsoft Edge has brought a tactical end to the famous IE. Adieu Internet Explorer; Adieu the most famous Web browser on earth.

In the view of the fact that Microsoft has chosen another favorite in the world of Web browsers, we have to put the past behind us and get connected with the new born. Edge browser is the new born and we all have to know how to get started with it.

However, this does not mean that Internet Explorer is not on your Windows 10 device. It is definitely still part of the Windows 10 ecosystem, and since your device is running Windows 10, you can be sure that this browser is on your device. But you will not find it on the taskbar nor the Start menu. You may need to use the search bar before you can find it.

As far as Microsoft is concerned, Edge browser is the new browser of choice. It is much simpler and faster. In addition, Edge browser makes it possible for you to write on Webpages and save it on OneNote or share it with your loved ones through emails. That is great; isn't it?

This comprehensive guide attempts to present Edge browser in a very clear and definitive manner so that both newbies and tech expert can get delighted reading it.

So let get started!

Opening the Edge Browser

The first thing you will need to do to access all the goodies that come with Microsoft Edge is to open it. This can be done by simply clicking on the **e** icon (a blue lowercase button) located on the taskbar.

Hint: There is cool way to open the Edge browser from any File Explorer Windows's address bar. This is particularly faster if you are already doing something on the File Explorer and you quickly want to check for a webpage. Just type the Web address of the page you want to visit into the File Explorer window's address bar and hit **Enter** on the keyboard. For example, type wikipedia.com into a File Explorer window's address bar and hit **Enter** to open the Wikipedia page. See the screenshot below.

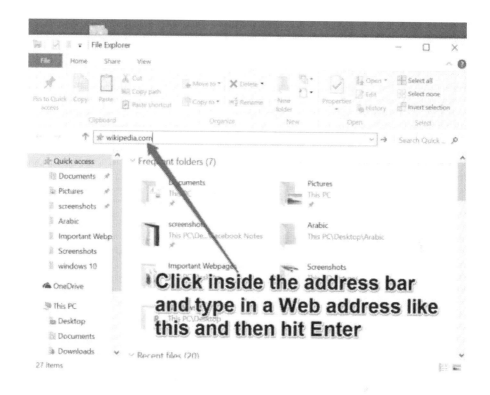

Please note that this command may not respond fast enough and it may take more than 5 seconds before the command get executed.

Get to know the Edge Browser Interface

The following screenshot will introduce you to various features found on Edge browser:

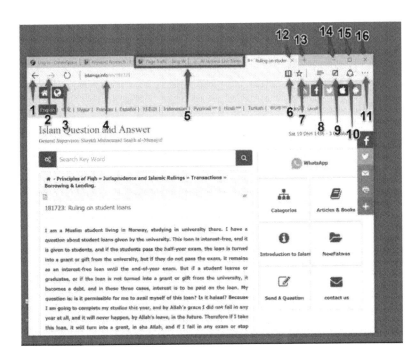

Islam Question and Answer

General Supervision: Shaykh Muhammad Saalih al-Munajjid

Search Key Word

 # - Principles of Fiqh » Jurisprudence and Islamic Rulings » Transactions » Borrowing & Lending.

181723: Ruling on student loans

I am a Muslim student living in Norway, studying in university there. I have a question about student loans given by the university. This loan is interest-free, and it is given to students, and if the students pass the half-year exam, the loan is turned into a grant or gift from the university, but if they do not pass the exam, it remains as an interest-free loan until the end-of-year exam. But if a student leaves or graduates, or if the loan is not turned into a grant or gift from the university, it becomes a debt, and in these three cases, interest is to be paid on the loan. My question is: is it permissible for me to avail myself of this loan? Is it halaal? Because I am going to complete my studies this year, and by Allah's grace I did not fail in any year at all, and it will never happen, by Allah's leave, in the future. Therefore if I take this loan, it will turn into a grant, in sha Allah, and if I fail in any exam or stop

WhatsApp

Categories

Articles & Books

Introduction to Islam

NewFatwas

Send A Question

contact us

4

1	**Back: Click this icon to revisit the page you just visited.**
2	**Forward**: Click this icon to return to the page you just left.
3	**Refresh**: Clicking this icon reloads a webpage.
4	**Address bar**: Clicking this bar let you enter the web address of a page. You may also type in search phrase into the address bar.
5	**Tabs:** Click this to navigate between different webpages.
6	**Reading View:** Click this icon to get a page that is customized for reading. The reading view removes the ads and unnecessary information making it easier to read a webpage.
7	**Add to Favorite or Reading List:** Click this icon to add a webpage to your favorite or to add a webpage to your reading list so that you can read it later.
8	**Hub:** This tab gives you access to your reading list, favorites, histories, and downloaded files.
9	**Web note**: Clicking this icon enables you to annotate a webpage and save it on OneNote or share it with friends.
10	**Share**: Click on this icon to share a webpage with loved ones.
11	**More Actions tab:** Click on this icon to access more options on Edge browser.
12	**Close tab:** Click this to close a tab.
13	**Add new tab**: Click this to add another webpage.
14	**Minimize Edge browser to the taskbar:** Click this icon to reduce the browser to an icon on the taskbar.

15	**Minimize/Maximize Edge browser window**: Click this icon to reduce or enlarge the size of Edge Window.
16	**Close Edge browser window**: Click this icon to close the Edge browser and close all the opened tabs. Microsoft Edge browser will usually warn you when closing all tabs.

Hint: If you mistakenly click or tap a wrong button, don't panic, just keep holding your finger or mouse pointer on the wrong button and then stylishly wove away your finger/mouse (just as if you are dragging the wrong icon) to stop the command from executing. Generally, command don't get executed until you release you finger or mouse pointer.

Customizing the Startup Page

The startup page is the page that opens when you just open your Edge browser. When you open the Edge browser, what you will see can either be the start page, a blank page or a custom page. This all depends on the default setting or what you have told your browser to do. Fortunately, you can choose how this page is displayed to you.

I can't vividly recollect the startup page that comes with Edge browser when I started using it. It is quite long ago. But whether I remember what the default startup page was or not, the most important is that you can change the way your startup page looks like. You may choose to change the default startup page by following the steps below:

- Open then **More actions (...)** tab and click on **Settings**

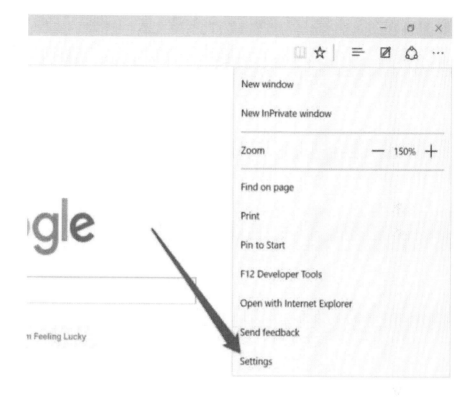

- Choose any of the following options under the **Open with** tab

- **Start page:** When you choose this option, Microsoft displayed news on your startup page. This news is powered by MSN.

- **New tap page:** If you want Edge browser not to display anything on your startup page then choose this option.

- **Previous pages:** When this option is chosen, your browser will load the pages you were viewing when last you closed it.

- **A specific page or pages:** This option is perfect for displaying your favorite webpages on the startup page. You can choose to display one or more custom pages. For example, you can choose to display Wikipedia, WordPress and Google on your startup. To select a webpage of your choice, select **Custom** from the drop-down menu under **A specific page or pages** and then enter webpage of your own. See the screenshot below.

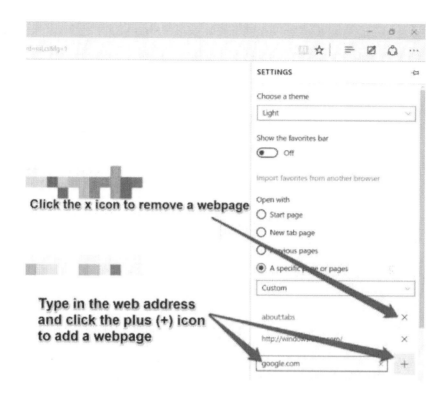

Click the x icon to remove a webpage

Type in the web address
and click the plus (+) icon
to add a webpage

Hint: You can choose the webpage you see first on the startup page by rearranging the custom webpages you have entered. To do this, navigate to the **custom** webpage settings page has shown above, and then drag things up and down in the list.

Using the Address/Search Bar

Every web browser must have an address bar and Edge browser also has one. This bar serves the function of URL address bar and search bar. By default, the searches done on this bar is executed by Bing. To learn how to change the search engine to Google, please go to page 25.

You choose whether to launch a webpage or search for a term based on what you type into the address bar.

For example, if you type **Windows Radar** into the address bar and press **Enter**, Bing search results for that phrase is displayed. On the other hand, if you type windowsradar.com and hit **Enter**, you will be taken to the website bearing the name.

Hint: To gain access to address bar straight away when using the Edge browser, Press **Ctrl + L** or **Alt + D.**

Furthermore you don't have to type in the .com part of a URL, you can just type in the name (omit both the www and .com parts) and press **Ctrl + Enter**. For example, to go to Wikipedia, type in **Wikipedia** into the address bar and press **Ctrl + Enter.**

Edge browser makes website suggestions to you based on the sites you have recently visited, to choose any of this suggested site, use the arrow key on the keyboard or the mouse to navigate the suggested sites and press **Enter** when you find the right one.

When you begin to type inside the address bar, Edge browser automatically makes suggestions beneath your typing. You can choose one of these suggestions to make things faster, provided that the suggestions truly read your mind.

In addition, you can choose to turn off the auto-suggestions feature by going to the Edge browser **Settings** and clicking on the **View advanced settings** (the last item on the list). Then click **Off** next to **Show search suggestions as I type**.

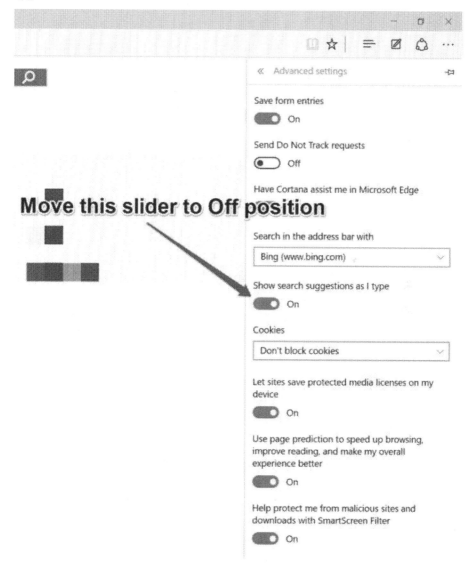

Controlling How You See the Webpages -- Using the Microsoft Edge Themes

Although not very robust, Microsoft Edge comes with themes. Basically, you can choose between two themes when using the browser. I will like to believe that Microsoft will make more themes available with time.

The default theme that comes with Edge browser is light theme but you may change this to black by following the steps below:

1. Open the **Settings** tab.

2. Click on the drop-down menu under **Choose a theme** and select **Dark**

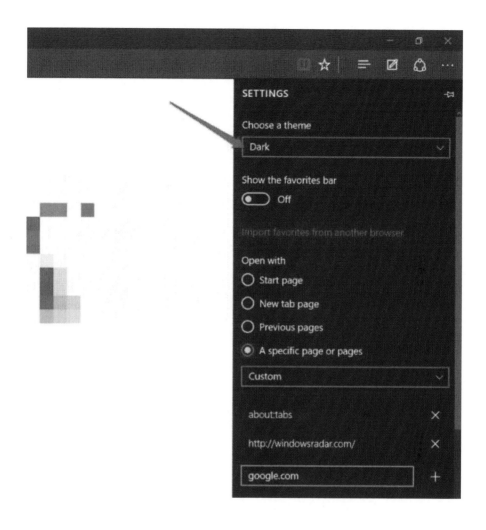

Navigating a Webpage- Scrolling Up/Down Smartly

When you open a long webpage, you will definitely have to scroll up and down. The traditional way to scroll a webpage is to use the mouse to move the slider, but there is a smarter way to do this. When next you want to scroll up, press **Page Up** or **Page Down** on the keyboard to scroll up or down respectively. In addition, you can use the arrow keys to scroll up/down. Pressing **Shift** + **Space bar** will also scroll up a webpage.

Zooming a Webpage in Edge Browser

To zoom a webpage in Microsoft Edge, press **Ctrl** and + key to zoom in and press **Ctrl** and - key to zoom out. Alternatively, open the **More actions (...)** tab and click on **Zoom.**

Using tabs on Edge browser

The tabs allow you to open different webpages at once. You can open many tabs at once on Edge browser. You can navigate different opened webpages by clicking the tabs above the window of these webpages. Please see the screenshot under **Get to know the Edge Browser Interface** to have a pictorial view of Edge browser tabs.

You can use the following keyboard shortcuts to manage tabs:

- **Ctrl** + **T**: Open a new tab

- **Ctrl** + **W**: Close a tab

- **Ctrl** + **Tab:** switch from one tab to the next

- **Ctrl** + **K**: Open a new duplicate tab of the tab you are presently viewing

- In addition you can move straight to a tab by pressing **Ctrl** and the number of the tab. For example, to move to the fourth tab press **Ctrl** + **4**

- To open a link in a separate tab, press **Ctrl** and that link.

What of the Home Button?

You might have asked yourself at one time or the other the location of home button when using the Edge browser. Fortunately for the Home button fans, there is a Home button in the Microsoft Edge. However, you will need to tell the browser that you want to see it before it can be displayed to you.

To show the Home button in your browser:

1. Click on the **More actions (...)** tab

2. Click on **Settings**

3. Click on the **View Advanced settings**

4. Next to **Show the home button** select **On**

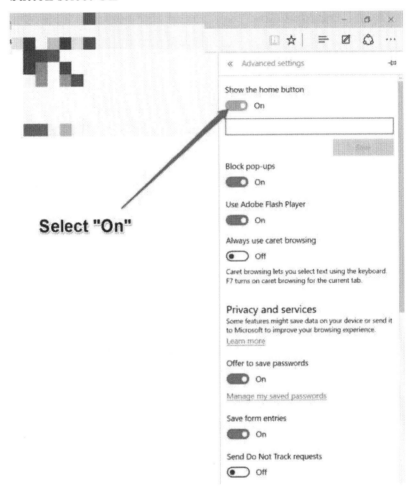

Select "On"

5. Type a webpage address in the space provided and click **Save.** If you type in a webpage address, the Edge browser will open this webpage whenever you click the home button.

Favorites (Bookmarks)

With several billions of webpages in the internet world, you just have to select your favorites. Just like other modern day browsers, Microsoft Edge gives you the opportunity to select a favorite or bookmark a page. This makes it easier to visit the website or webpage in the future.

To add a website to favorites:

1. Open the website you want to bookmark

2. Press **Ctrl + D**. Alternatively, you may click on the favorite icon on the address bar. See the screenshot below:

3. Tab in the **Name** you want.

4. Click **Add.**

Accessing Your Favorites

After you have added a webpage to your favorites list, you will need to access this list sooner or later. To access the favorite list, press **Ctrl + I**. Alternatively you may click the **Hub** icon and then click on Favorites icon.

What about the favorite bar

The favorite bar is the favorite panel beneath the address bar. This bar is not there by default and you will need to activate it yourself if you want it. Displaying the favorite tab allows you to access your most used webpages with just a single click.

There are two ways to make the Favorites bar appear on your browser. The first and faster way is to click **Ctrl + Shift + B**. To remove the Favorites tab, press this command again.

The second way is to go to your Edge browser's **Settings** and select **On** under **Show the favorites tab.**

Hint: You can rearrange how the webpages appear on your favorite bar. To do this, click and drag a webpage on the favorite bar to left or right.

Importing your bookmarks from other browsers

When you start using the Edge browser, you will like to import your bookmarks from other browsers. To import your bookmarks to Edge browser:

1. Press **Ctrl + I** to access the Favorites tab

2. Click on **Import favorites**

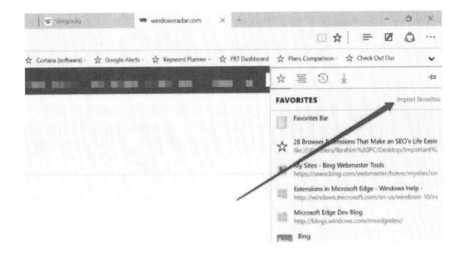

3. Select browsers from the list and click on **Import** (See the screenshot below)

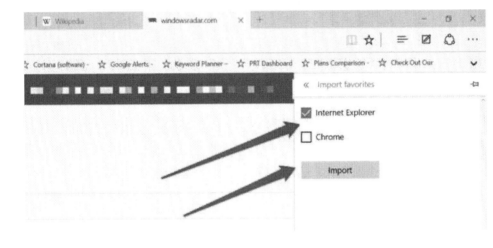

Managing the Reading List

Webpages contain a lot of information and you will probably need to schedule some webpages for later reading. Microsoft Edge reading list is a great way to do this. When you find and interesting information online and you don't have the time to read it now, you can save it for later reading by keeping it in your reading list.

The reading list is one of the features under the **hub** tab.

The fastest way to access the reading list is by pressing **Ctrl + G.** Alternatively, a slower way will be to click on the **Hub** icon and then click the reading list icon.

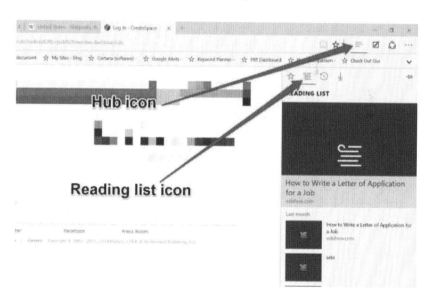

To add a webpage to the reading list, open the webpage and click on the star icon as though you are about to add a Favorite. In the dialog box that appears, select **Reading list** tab. Edit the name, if you like, and click on **Add.**

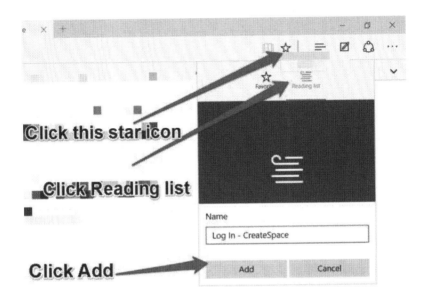

Alternatively, you may press **Ctrl + D** and select **Reading list** and then select **Add.**

Downside: It appears that Reading list in Edge browser is not very robust as I would have love. Although Microsoft Edge saves the web-address, it appears that it does not actually store the Web pages on your PC so that you can read them offline later. This mean that you will still need internet connection to read the webpages in your reading list.

Understanding the Edge Browser Reading View

The Edge reading browser reading view allows you to read a webpage in an optimized way. The reading view is customized for better reading. It gives you access to just text and images on a webpage eliminating adds and other unnecessary information on a webpage.

To activate the reading view on a webpage, press **Ctrl + Shift + R.** Alternatively, you can click on the reader button on the address bar. To exit the reading view, click the reading view button again or press **Ctrl + Shift + R**

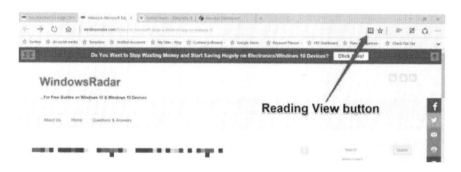

Note: Not all webpages are supported by the reading view; the reading view icon will appear bold if the webpage you are viewing is supported.

Customizing the reading view

You can make some tweaks to reading view by going to the settings. To customize the reading view, click on **More actions (...)** button and select **Settings**. Then select the any of the following options under the **Reading** tab:

- **Reading view style:** Under this option you can select any of the following:

1.   Default

2.   Light

3.   Medium

4.   Dark

- **Reading view font size:** You can choose any of the following:

1.   Small

2.   Medium

3.   Large

4.   Extra Large

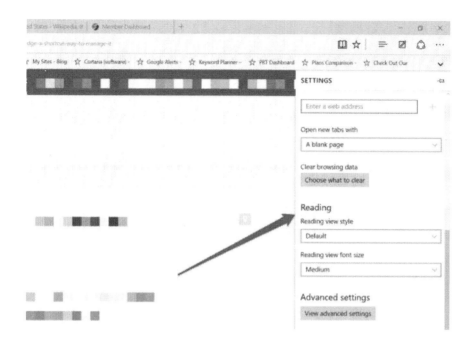

Changing the Search Engine

The default search engine on Microsoft Edge is Bing. Many people will love to change this to Google.

You can change the Microsoft Edge Search Engine (Bings) to Google by following the steps highlighted below:

1. While the browser is opened, click on menu icon and select **Settings**.

Click **View advanced settings**.

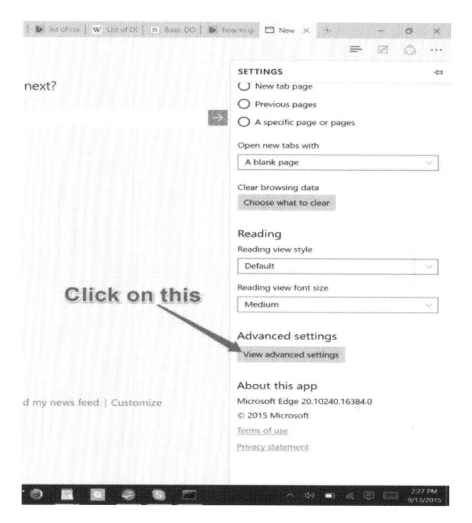

3. Click on drop-down menu under **Search in the address bar with** and select Google if it is present in the list. If not, select **Add new**. After you have added Google (if necessary) click on **Add as default** to make Google your default search engine on Microsoft Edge.

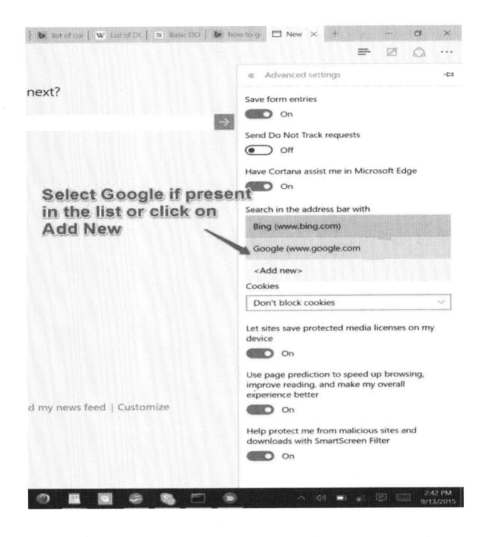

The Edge Browser Caret Browsing

Don't mind the technical jargon, caret browsing is simply a feature that allows you to use the keyboard to select text and navigate a webpage.

Basically it involves using these five options to control a webpage. These keyboard buttons are

1. Pressing the **Home** key to take you to the top of a webpage

2. Pressing the **End** key to take you to the end of a webpage

3. Pressing the **PageDown** key to scroll down a webpage

4. Pressing the **PageUp** key to scroll up a webpage

5. Using the **Shift** key and the arrow key to select text on a webpage

You can either choose to be able to use these keyboard buttons to navigate a webpage or not, and that is the whole idea of caret browsing. When the Caret browsing option is switched **On**, you will be able to use these keyboard buttons mentioned above to control a webpage.

To turn On the Caret browsing:

1. Open the **More actions (...)** tab

2. Click on **Settings**

3. Click on **Advanced Settings**

4. Under **Always use the caret browsing** choose **On**

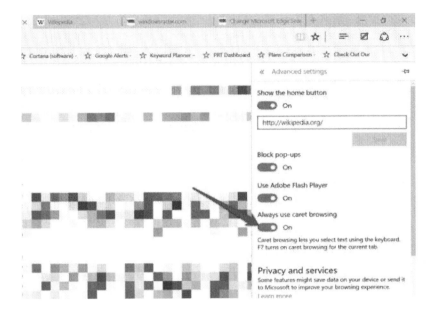

Note: As at the time of writing this guide, it appears that switching the caret button on or off does not affect the caret browsing on the Edge browser. I am not sure if this is a bug with my Edge browser. If you are experiencing the same thing, please let me know using my email.

Managing the History List

Edge browser collects the history of the webpages you visit and stores it.

There are many ways you can manage Microsoft Edge browsing history, but some ways are smarter than others.

In this section of the guide, I will tell you a smart way to quickly manage your browsing history.

You can manage your Edge history smartly with these three keyboard shortcuts:

1. Use **Ctrl + H** to access browsing history from any tab in Microsoft Edge Browser. By just pressing these two keys, you will have the browsing history opened before you.

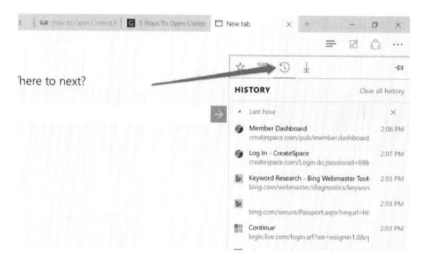

2. Use **Ctrl + J** to access Edge browser download history. Press this two keys and gain access to all your past downloads.

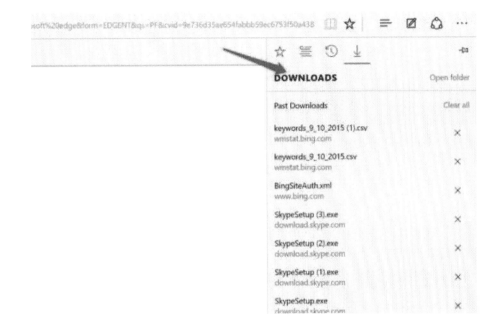

3. Use **Ctrl + Shift + Delete** to access **Clear browsing data** page and clear your browsing history.

Using Cortana on Edge Browser

Cortana is probably the most famous feature on Windows 10 and you can be sure that it is also integrated with Microsoft Edge.

Cortana is a voice-controlled personal assistant on Windows 10. With some text command you can activates this feature.

While using your Edge browser, you can use Cortana in the following ways:

- **Address bar search**: When you type in some specific phrase into the address bar on Edge browser, you can put Cortana to work. For example to check the weather of New York type in **Weather 10024**. This will give you the New York weather information even before you press **Enter** key.

- **More info about a phrase**: If you are reading an article and you encounter a word or phrase that is difficult, you can quickly ask Cortana. Just select the text and right click on it. Then choose **Ask Cortana.** See the red arrow.

Using the Web Note

Microsoft is very proud of the fact that Edge browser allows you to annotate a Webpage. To the best of my knowledge, as at the time of writing this guide, it is the only modern day browser that gives you that opportunity.

To annotate a webpage:

- Open the webpage and click on the Markup button in the top-right corner of Edge browser.

- Use the following tools to get a beautiful annotation:

1. **Pan**: This tool allows you to move the web page so as to see other part of the webpage. To pan, just select this tool and then click and drag in various directions.

2. **Pen:** Use this just like you will use your pen. When you click the pen icon tip, you are given the option of chosen the color and the size/pen thickness. You can use the Surface pen that came with your device to make annotations as you like.

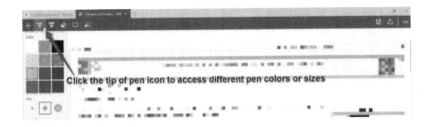

Click the tip of pen icon to access different pen colors or sizes

3. **Highlighter:** Think of this as a marker you use on paper. You can use the highlighter button to highlight a text so as to pay special attention to it. Just like pen tool, you can also select the color or size of the highlighter by clicking on the tip of the highlighter tool icon.

4. **Eraser:** Every writer needs an eraser, and you surely also need one. Edge browser gives you the opportunity to erase a markup in case you make a mistake. You can erase all you annotations by clicking on the tip of eraser icon and selecting **Clear all ink**.

5. **Typed notes:** This looks like a comment box. When you click this icon and then click any part of a webpage, a little box appears to let you add special note to the webpage. You can move the typed note by dragging its handle. You can also minimize a typed note by clicking on the handle just once. To delete a typed note, click on the **Delete icon**. The typed note box automatically increase in size to accommodate new notes as you type in more words.

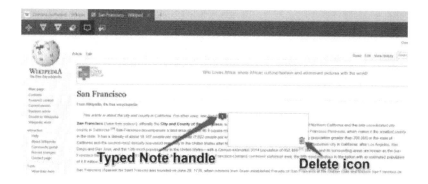

Typed Note handle

Delete icon

6. **Clip:** This is similar to what we have in other image editors. You can use this tool to copy a part of a webpage. When you click this icon, you will be asked to drag to copy a region of a webpage. When you drag the rectangular box and release it, this webpage is copied to your clipboard. You can then paste it to Microsoft Word or other similar programs by pressing **Ctrl + V**.

Export/Saving a Web Note

After spending sometime annotating a webpage, you will need to save it to avoid losing your work. When you click the Save button, you will have the chance to save your work to the following places:

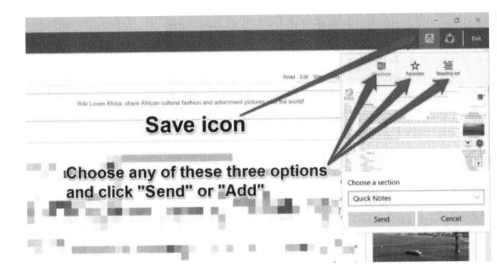

- **OneNote**: You can choose this option to have your annotation stored as a note in OneNote.

- **Favorites:** You can choose to save your markup as a favorite. You can also save the web note in a new favorite folder by clicking the **Create new Folder.** In addition, you can type a name for your annotated webpage before saving it in favorites.

- **Reading List:** Similar to Favorites you can also save the markup as one of the items on your reading list. You can type a name for your annotated webpage before saving it in reading list.

Notes:

- When a markup is saved to Favorite or Reading List. You can choose to hide annotation when viewing it by clicking on **Hide.**

- Although you have the opportunity to edit the web note when you save it in reading list or favorites, it appears that you will need to save another copy of this web note after you are done editing. Edge browser will not replace your web note with the new edited version.

Sharing Your Web Note with Friends

To share your web note with friends or email it to someone, click on the **Share** button located beside the save button. Then choose a social media from the sharing options that appear.

Closing the Web Note

When you are done with making a web note, click on **Exit**

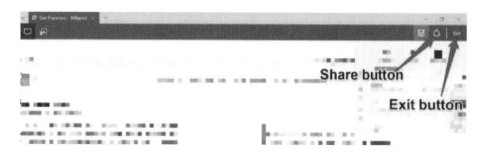

Printing Web Pages on Microsoft Edge

Printing on Microsoft Edge is quite fantastic. I love the fact that Edge browser neatly fit a webpage within a page. You can initiate the printing process by pressing **Ctrl + P**. Alternatively, you can click on **More actions** (...) tab and select **Print.**

You can use these various options on the print window to customize what comes out of your printer. These Options include:

- **Orientation**: This option allows you to choose between portrait and landscape.

- **Pages:** Choose between printing the current page or just enter the range of pages to print. You can also print all pages by selecting **All.**

- **Scale**: Use this option to tell the printer whether to shrink the web pages to fit or choose from scaling options. Choosing a lower scaling option like 50% allows you to save paper because more words will be printed per page. However, the fonts may be too small if you choose a small scaling option.

- **Margins**: Use this option to tell your printer which margin to leave on the paper. You can choose between normal, narrow, moderate, or wide. Choosing a narrow margin will ensure that you print more words per page and thereby save paper.

- **Header and footers**: Use this option to tell your printer whether to include URL of the web page and the name of the Web page in the header and the footer.

- **More settings:** This gives you access to **paper size and quality** and **page layout.**

It is important to mention that some webpages give you the opportunity to print their web information by clicking on Print icon located on their webpages. When you have a situation like this, I will advise that you print the webpage using the Print icon located on the webpage. This is because a website's print feature usually eliminates ads and other unnecessary information from a print page making sure that the printout will not be chopped off or distorted.

Edge InPrivate Browsing

There are times when you will not want your browser to save any information about your visit to a Web page, and InPrivate browsing is good for a time like this. To activate InPrivate browsing, click the **More actions** (...) button and select New InPrivate window.

How to Pin a Menu in the Edge Browser

When you access the Microsoft Edge settings, you will realize that it normally covers a sizable part of a webpage, to eliminate this constraint and make sure that the settings tab is easily accessible, I will advise that you Pin the Settings menu to the browser. To do this open the settings tab and click on the pin icon located on the settings pane.

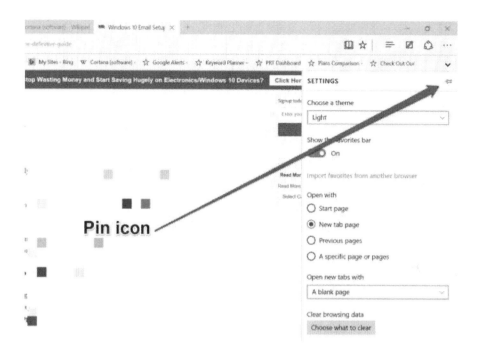

Please note that you can also pin other items like the reading list and favorites to the Edge browser. Just click on the pin icon as described above.

More on Edge Browser Settings

Many options under Edge Settings have already been discussed but there are some that I will like to mention.

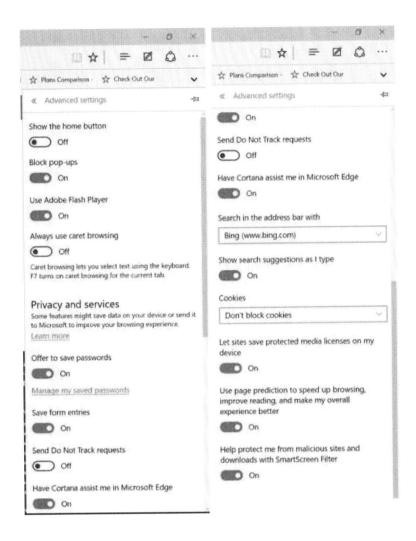

1. **Block pop-ups:** This option allows you to block websites from opening a pop-up window.

2. **Use Adobe Flash Player:** Enabling this option makes it possible to play the video contents of many websites.

3. **Offer to save passwords**: You probably have tens of different passwords. You can use this Edge feature to allow

the browser to offer to save your password whenever you enter a password or login information in a new website. In addition, click on **Manage my saved passwords** to make changes to your saved passwords.

4. **Save form entries:** Use this option to enable Microsoft Edge to save your form entries whenever you fill in information into an online form.

5. **Do not send track request**: Use this option to discourage websites from tracking you.

6. **Have Cortana assist me in Microsoft Edge**: Use this option to enable Cortana to work with Edge browser.

7. **Let sites save protected media licenses on my device:** Use this option to allow website to save a licensed media materials on your Windows 10 device.

8. **Use page prediction to speed up browsing, improve reading, and make my overall experience better:** Edge browser will speed up your browsing experience if this option is enabled.

9. **Help protect me from malicious sites and downloads with SmartScreen Filter:** SmartScreen filters is a feature that protects you from phishing websites and malicious software. I will advise that you always keep this feature **On**.

More on the More actions (...) tab

Many options under the More actions (...) tab have already been discussed, but I will like to explain the remaining items that have not already been discussed.

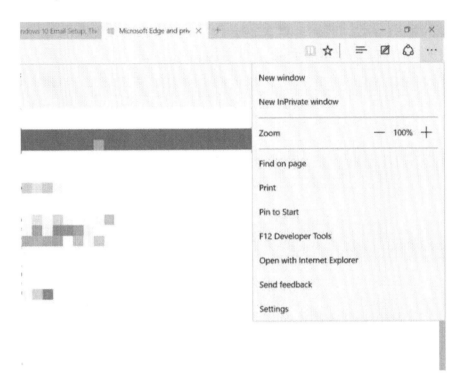

1. **Zoom**: Use this option to zoom in or zoom out a webpage.

2. **Find on page:** Use this option to search for a word or a phrase on a webpage.

3. **Pin to Start:** Use this option to pin a webpage to the start.

4. **F12 Developer Tools:** Use this option to access Microsoft Edge developer tools. This is useful for programmers.

5. **Open with Internet Explorer:** You can open a webpage in Internet explorer by clicking this option.

6. **Send feedback:** Use this option to report an issue to Microsoft.

What about Microsoft Edge Extensions

Extensions open a new world for many internet users. Unfortunately as at the time of writing this guide, Microsoft has not made available extensions in Edge browser.

However, Microsoft is working seriously on making the extensions available in no time and I expect it to be available in some weeks' time.

How to Save a Webpage for Offline Use in Microsoft Edge

Unfortunately the usual **Ctrl + S** is not working on Edge browser. In fact, if you save a webpage in reading list, you will still need an internet access to read it. This means that there is no direct way to save a web page for offline reading in Edge browser.

Fortunately, there is a way round this problem. To save a webpage for offline reading:

1. Click the Web Note icon.

2. Click Save icon.

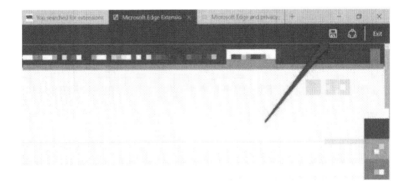

3. Choose either Favorites, Reading list or OneNote and then click on **Send/Add**

How to download a file in Edge browser

1. Open the webpage

2. Locate and click on the download link

3. Wait for the download to finish and click on **Open**

Please note that if you are downloading a pdf document, it will automatically open with the Edge browser pdf reader.

You can pause a download by clicking on **Pause** while the file is still downloading. Please note that to use this option the file will still need to be downloading. If the file has finished downloading the **Pause** button will not be available.

What about the Edge Browser PDF Reader.

Just like many modern day Web browsers, Microsoft Edge has an inbuilt PDF Reader. To use the Edge PDF Reader, right click on the document that you want to read and select **Open with.** Then select **Microsoft Edge**.

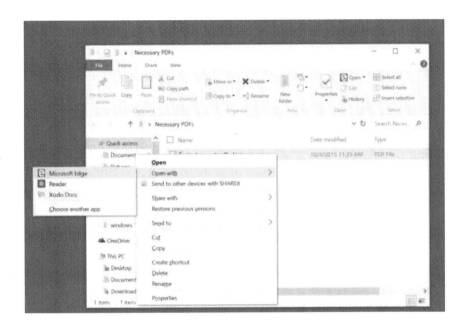

The Shortcut keys in the Edge browser

Many keyboard shortcuts have already been mentioned in this guide but I still wish to mention new ones and re-mention some.

Press **Ctrl** + **T** to open a new tab

Press **Ctrl** + **H** to access browsing history in Edge browser.

Press **Ctrl** + **J** to access Microsoft Edge download history.

Press **Ctrl** + **P** to print a page

Press **Ctrl** + **N** to open a new Window

Press **Ctrl** + **F** to find any word or phrase on a webpage

Press **Ctrl** + **D** to add a page to Favorite list.

Press **Ctrl** + **Shift** + **Delete** to access Clear browsing data page. This will allow you to quickly clear your browsing data.

Troubleshooting Edge Browser

Being an app, Edge browser may sometime refuse to work properly or it may hang. If this happens, just close the browser and open it again. If the browser refuses to close then

Press **Ctrl + Alt + Delete** and choose **Task Manager** from the dialog box that appears. Then right click on **Microsoft Edge** and choose **End task.**

Conclusion

Edge Browser is a new comer to world of Web browsers and there are still many things that Microsoft still needs to improve. That being said, I strongly believe that this guide will help you with this browser so that you can use it like a pro.

Cortana

Introduction

Cortana is a trained virtual assistant that has been built to answer questions, and interestingly, you probably don't need any technical training to use this feature. If you need any, it will be some tweaks and how to ask question and that is what this section of the guide is mainly for. This section of the guide will show you how to manage Cortana like a pro and how to ask questions and give commands that Cortana will understand.

The question can either be asked by speech or by typing it. This makes it more cool, you don't need to worry too much that it will not understand your bass voice.

In addition, you will be using this feature at one time or the other while using you're your device, and that is why you need a guide like this to get you started.

This unofficial guide attempts to present Cortana in an understandable and direct manner so that you can use this feature like a pro.

So let get started!

Getting started with Cortana

You will need to setup Cortana when you first start using you're your device and you will learn how to do that in this section of the guide. To setup the voice assistant:

1. Click in the search box. A **Privacy Statement** will appear telling you which information Cortana will collect from you and how this information will be used. I will advise that you carefully read this Privacy Statement so as to know which information is collected.

2. If you are satisfied with the Privacy Statement, click **I agree,** if not, click **No thanks.** If you click **No thanks,** you don't need to read this guide further because you will not be able to use Cortana. If you agree to the privacy statement then go to the next step below.

3. Cortana will then ask to choose a name to call you. Type your name and click **Next.** Please note that you may also skip this step if you don't want Cortana to address you by name.

Note: Although you have to agree to the Cortana's privacy statement during the set up process, you can always choose how Cortana access your information. For example, you can do adjust some settings under Notebook to limit the amount of information Cortana sends to Microsoft. Please read the information written in italics on page 74 to find out more.

Speaking to Cortana

One of the ways you will interact with Cortana is by speaking to her. The other way will be to just type command into the search bar and hit **Enter**. There are few things to know when talking to Cortana so as to get the best experience.

To get Cortana into action, you will need to get her attention. To do that, please follow the steps below:

1. Press **Windows key** + **C.** This will open the Cortana Listening box. You can then ask her any question you want.

2. Alternatively, you can get Cortana's attention by saying **Hey Cortana.** However, you will need to enable this feature before you can put it to use. To enable **Hey Cortana** function:

- Click the search box on the Start menu. Then click on **Notebook** icon.

- Click the **Settings.**

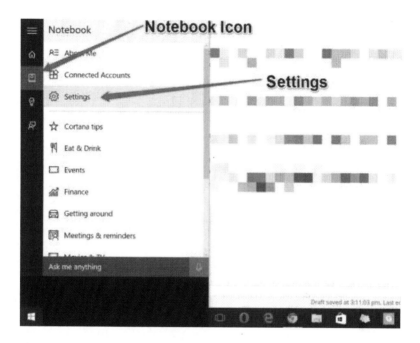

- Next to **Hey Cortana,** select **On**

3. Lastly, you can get Cortana's attention by clicking the microphone button on the start menu.

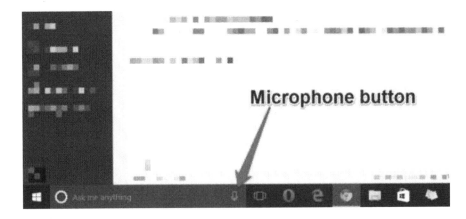

When Cortana is activated she will respond by saying **Listening** in the search box. Then speak your question to her. As you ask a question or give a command, blocks of random alphabet letters will begin to show in the search box and they will merge to form words. This is the words you have spoken to Cortana, and she will then give you an answer on the search box immediately or open your web browser. By default Cortana will search the web using Bing but you can always change this to Google. Please go to page 79 to know more.

In addition, you may notice that the question you asked Cortana is different from what she types into the search box (what Cortana types into the search box is what she thought you have said), I will advise that you should not bother yourself much about this as Microsoft claims that Cortana is programmed to learn from you as time goes on. You can also train Cortana to learn your voice, please go to page 76 to know how to get started.

What about Typing

The interesting thing is that Cortana can also listen when you command it using your keyboard. You can type in command and get a similar result just as you will get by speaking to her. This is a great feature especially if you can't speak to Cortana for one reason or the other e.g. if you are in a noisy place or your microphone is not working properly.

For example, you can get a result of what Cortana can do for you by typing **What can I say** into the search box (located on the start menu) and then hit **Enter**. This is similar to the result you will get when you say **What can I say** to Cortana.

Getting What You Want From Cortana

There are many things you can ask Cortana to do for you and before you finish reading this guide you will learn how to effectively interact with her.

I will like to mention that interacting with Cortana is not an examination (so there is nothing like cheating) and you can always get a list of what she can do for you by typing or speaking **What can I say** or **What can you do** and then clicking a category from the list that appears.

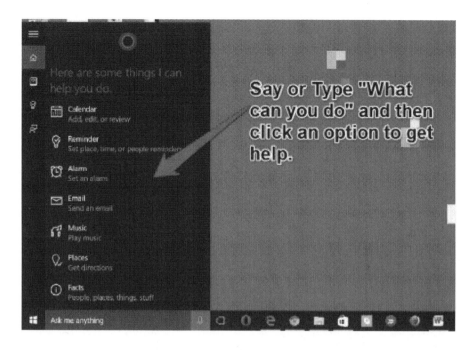

If you are speaking to her please don't forget that you will first need to press the microphone button as described in the section above. Alternatively, if you have enabled the feature, you may also say **Hey Cortana** to get her attention. Asking "what can I say" is a good way to help yourself anytime get stuck on how to use this virtual assistant.

Using Cortana to open Apps or Programs

One of those things you will want to use Cortana to do is access your apps. You can quickly open an app by saying **Open** and then mentioning the name of the app. For example, to open Settings, say or type **Open settings.** To open calculator, say **Open calculator**.

You may also say **Launch settings** instead of **Open settings.**

In addition, you may give a more specific command like **Open notification settings** to go to notification settings. Say **Launch Wi-Fi Settings** to open the Wi-Fi settings. To turn on airplane mode, say **Turn on airplane mode** and so on.

Using Cortana with Calendar

One of the fantastic features that Cortana can do for you is making an appointment. This personal assistant is fully integrated with your device's Calendar making it easy for her to make appointments for you.

With just few commands you can get Cortana to put an event or appointment into your calendar. To do this:

1. Press **Windows Key** + **C** or click the microphone icon on the search bar to get Cortana's attention. She will respond by typing **listening** in the search box.

2. Then say whatever you want to include in the Calendar. For example, you can say the following:

    - Appointment with Clinton for Monday at 1 p.m.

    - Be in a conference with John at 10 a.m. on Sunday

- Fixed my car at 5 p.m. tonight. Please note that you can also say all the examples given above in another ways, the most important thing is to get Cortana to understand what you are saying.

- When she has gotten the information, the calendar will appear on the start menu. You can then click on **Add** or say **Yes** if you are satisfied with the response. If not, say **No** or **Cancel.**

Good news: Cortana will inform you if your new appointment clashes with anyone already in your calendar so you don't have to worry about that.

You can also make changes to your calendar using Cortana. To do this:

1. Repeat the first step above.

2. Then say what you want her to change. For example, you may say any of the following:

    - Change the meeting schedule for 1 p.m. to 4 p.m.

    - Move my appointment from 5 p.m. to 7 p.m.

In addition, you can check how your calendar looks like today. To do this

Press the microphone button and say "**What is on my calendar today?**" Or say "**any appointment today**?" Or just any variant. Note that you can also ask Cortana about your calendar for a day in the future. To do this, say "**Any appointment tomorrow**" or say "**Any appointment on November 1st.**"

Note: In case, Cortana set a wrong appointment, you can edit it using your keyboard instead of trying to speak another word to her. Editing any misinformation with keyboard appears smarter and faster.

In addition, Instead of speaking, you may type any of the commands mentioned above into the search box to get a similar result.

Using Cortana to set Reminders

There are probably many things going through your mind and it will be quite interesting if you can get a personal assistant to assist in remembering some of your duties. Fortunately, Cortana can help you in this regard.

To set a reminder using Cortana:

1. Press **Windows Key + C** or click the microphone icon on the search bar to get Cortana's attention. She will respond by typing **listening** in the search box.

2. Then say whatever you want to set a reminder for. For example, you can say the following:

- Remind me to fix the car by 3 p.m.

- Remind to drop the cake at the restaurant.

- Remind me to pick my daughter at 4 p.m.

- Remind me to call Ibrahim at 1 p.m. and so on.

3. When she has gotten the information, the reminder will appear. You can then click on **Add** or say **Yes** if you are satisfied with the response. If not, say **No** or **Cancel.**

Please note that it is not compulsory that you put remind in every statement as I did above, but I will advise that you do this whenever you can. This is because it will help Cortana to easily get what you are saying and avoid any confusion.

Note: In case, Cortana set a wrong reminder, you can edit it using your keyboard instead of trying to speak another word to her. Editing any misinformation with keyboard appears smarter and faster.

Using Cortana with Alarm

You can also set an alarm using this personal assistant. To do this:

1. Repeat the first step mentioned above.

2. Say the time for alarm. For example you can say: "**set an alarm for 1 p.m. tomorrow**" or "**alarm for 1 p. m tomorrow**".

3. When she has gotten the information, the alarm will appear and she will tell you that she has set the alarm.

Using Cortana with Clock

You can ask Cortana what your local time is. In addition, it can also tell you the time in a specific place.

1. Press **Windows Key** + **C** or click the microphone icon on the search bar to get Cortana's attention. She will respond by typing **listening** in the search box.

2. Then say "**What is the time**" or say "**what is the time in New York**"

Using Cortana to Get Flight Information

You can also use this virtual assistant to get information about a flight. This is a smarter way to know when a particular airplane will take off.

For example you can say **Flight status of Delta 400** to get the flight information about this particular flight.

Using Cortana with Weather App

To know about your weather, just say **"What's the weather going to be today"**. You may also know about the weather condition of a place by asking **"What is the weather of New York today."**

Using Cortana with Mail App

You can instruct Cortana to compose an email for you. To do this:

1. Press **Windows Key** + **C** or click the microphone icon on the search bar to get Cortana's attention. She will respond by typing **listening** in the search box.

2. Then say the subject and the person you want to email. For example, you can say:

   - Email Clinton about the meeting

   - Email Clinton and Steve about the budget

   - Send Urgent email to Steve about the ball

The interesting thing is that you can type some of the commands given above into the search box and get similar results.

Please note that you will usually have to include one or more information before you send the email. For example, you may need to type the body of the email yourself. You can click **Continue in Outlook** link to finish the email process.

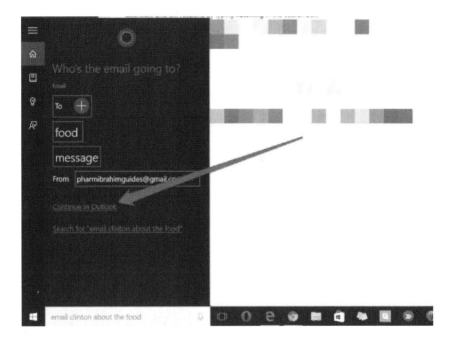

Using Cortana with Map App

You can also use the Cortana to search the map. This virtual assistant is fully integrated with the Map app on your device. To get how the map of a place looks like:

1. Repeat the first step above.

2. Then say the map of an area you want to get. For example, you may say:

- Map of Seattle

- show me the map of Seattle

What about Math?

Cortana can also help you with some mathematical and conversion. For example you can tell Cortana **"What is the square root of four"**. You may also say **"convert foot to centimeter"** or **"What is the exchange rate between dollars and pounds"** and so on. As I have said before, the most important thing is to make sure Cortana get the message you are trying to get across.

Using Cortana to get definitions

You can quickly check for a meaning of a word by asking Cortana. For example, you may say **"What is the meaning of flabbergasted"** or just say **"Meaning of flabbergasted"**

Note: Some time Cortana will display the answer of what you are asking for in your Web browser and not on the search pane.

Using Cortana with Microsoft Edge

You can also use this personal assistant when using your Microsoft Edge.

While using your Edge browser, you can use Cortana in the following ways:

- **Address bar search**: When you type in some specific phrase into the address bar on Edge browser, you can put Cortana to work. For example to check the weather of New York type in **Weather 10024.** This will give you the New York weather information even before you press **Enter** key.

- **More info about a phrase**: If you are reading an article and you encounter a word or phrase that is difficult, you can quickly ask Cortana. Just select the text and right click on it. Then choose **Ask Cortana.** See the red arrow.

Funny sides of Cortana

One of the main features that Microsoft is proud of in Cortana is her ability to give a reply in funny manner. This all depends on what you ask her. Some of the questions you can ask her to get funny replies are given below:

- Question: Do you sleep?

- Cortana: I never sleep, sleep is for ambulatory carbon-based being.

- Question: Do you eat?

- Cortana: I can only consume things that come in bytes.

- Question: Do you like your job?

- Cortana: I am tailor-made for this job.

- Question: Do you have a brain?

- Cortana: I am a cloud of infinitesimal computation, so I am anatomy-free.

- Question: Do you cook?

- Cortana: Even if I could, you would be smart not to eat it. I'm better at looking up recipes.

The list of questions you can ask Cortana to get funny replies goes on like that. As I have said before, it all depends on the type of question you ask this virtual machine sitting on your device.

Cortana's Card and the Notebook

The notebook is like a special note pad where Cortana stores information about you.

On the other hand, the Cortana card is what appears when you click the search box (before saying or typing anything). This usually includes news headlines, weather, restaurant recommendations and so on. An example of Cortana cards is shown below:

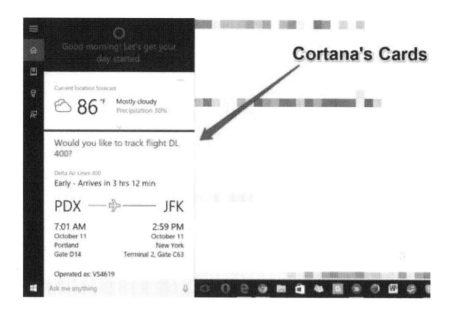

Cortana's Cards

Current location forecast

86 °F   Mostly cloudy
        Precipitation 30%

Would you like to track flight DL 400?

Delta Air Lines 400
Early - Arrives in 3 hrs 12 min

PDX ----✈---- JFK

7:01 AM   2:59 PM
October 11   October 11
Portland   New York
Gate D14   Terminal 2, Gate C63

Operated as: VS4619

Ask me anything

Hint: When viewing the Cortana's card in Cortana's pane, click on three dots icon (…) located beside the individual cards to quickly manage the settings. See the screenshot below.

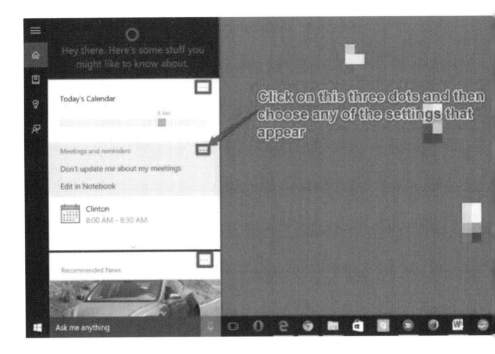

Interestingly, you can tell Cortana, how you want the cards to be displayed to you. You can customize which kind of cards appear in her panel. To do this, please follow the steps below:

1. Click the search box and click the Notebook icon.

2. Then click on any of the cards that you want to customize. These cards include:

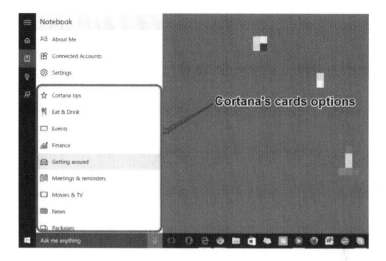

- **Cortana Tip**: Use this option to tell Cortana whether you want her to display tips to you when you get stuck when speaking to her.

- **Eat & Drink**: You can use this option to tell this virtual assistant what type of information to give you on food and drink.

- **Events**: Use this option to tell Cortana what you will like to know about local events.

- **Finance**: Use this option to tell Cortana which stock to track.

- **Getting around**: Use this option to manage your traffic.

Please note that there still more options under Cortana's card, and I will advise that you go through all of them individually to familiarize yourself with them. Most of the options under Cortana's card are self-explanatory and I believe you should get use to them easily.

*More importantly, if for one reason or the other, you don't want Cortana to get much information about you, then make sure you only turn **On** the features you are pleased with under the Cortana's card. Don't just turn **On** all the features if you don't need them.*

Others features in Cortana's Notebook

Other than Cortana's card, we have three more features under Cortana's notebook and they are

- **About Me**: Use this option to change the name Cortana calls you. You also have the option to enter your favorites under the favorite tab. The favorite tab allows you to enter information relating to places you visit often. Use the + icon to add favorites. When you are done with the settings under this tab, click the Notebook icon to go back to the Notebook settings.

- **Connected Account**: Use this option to connect **Office 365** (if you have one) so that Cortana can serve you better.

- **Settings**: check the next section for more information on this.

Cortana's Settings

The settings tab under Cortana's Notebook allows you to manage Cortana's functions. The settings include:

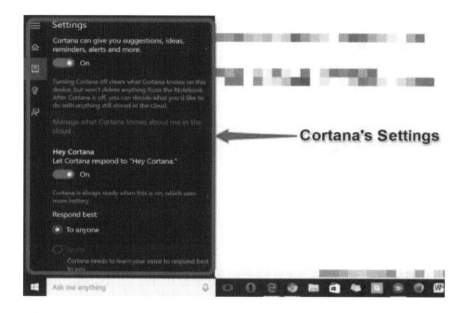

Cortana's Off/On Switch: Use this option to completely turn off Cortana. If this switch is moved to the **Off** position, you will not be able to use any of the Cortana's features.

Hey Cortana: Use this option to control whether Cortana will respond to **Hey Cortana.** When this feature is **On**, you will be able to get this virtual assistant attention by saying **Hey Cortana.** This feature appears cool but may also consume your device's battery. It is better off if you want to save battery power.

Respond best: Use this option to tell Cortana to respond to only you or just anyone. If you want Cortana to respond to just only you, then you have to train her to learn your voice by clicking **Learn my voice.** And then follow the on-screen instructions to finish the voice training.

Find flights and more: If this option is turned On, Windows will continuously monitor your Mail app to see if there is any flight and shipping information. This will enable her to alert you when there is one.

Taskbar tidbits: Use this option to control what appears on the search bar on the taskbar. Usually what is there by default is "**Ask me anything",** but you can use this tab to enable Cortana to change this to other cool statements from time to time.

Bing SafeSearch Settings: Click on this option to manage Bing search settings.

Other Privacy settings: Use this option to get access to extra privacy options

*Note: If for one reason or the other, you don't want Cortana to get much information about you, then make sure you only turn **On** the features/settings you are pleased with.*

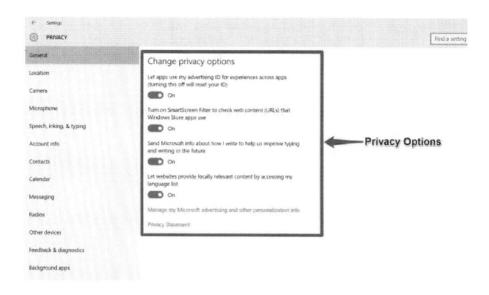

Privacy Options

Learn more about Cortana & Search: Click on this option to get access to **Cortana, Search, and privacy: FAQ** webpage

How to Completely Clear Cortana History (Stored Information)

To delete whatever information Cortana has stored on your device, switch off this virtual assistant. To completely switch off Cortana, click on the notebook icon and then click on **Settings.** Under **Cortana gives you suggestions, ideas, reminders, and more** choose **Off.**

Please note that you will also need to erase whatever Cortana has stored in the cloud to ensure that you have completely cleared Cortana's history. To this, click on the link "**Manage what Cortana knows about me in the cloud.**"

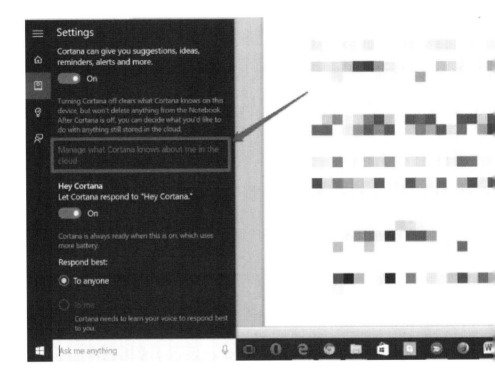

When you click on this link, you may get the message that the webpage you are trying to access does not exist. I am not sure why this happens, but I expect Microsoft to fix the issue soon.

Forcing Cortana to Use Other Browsers

By default Cortana is customized to use Edge browser to search for information online, but there is a way to change these settings. To do this:

1. Type "**Default app**" into the search bar on the start menu and press **Enter**

2. Scroll down until you find **Web browser**, click on this and select Firefox or just any other browser from the list.

Changing the Cortana and Bing partnership

By default Cortana uses Bing to search for information online, but you can force her to use Google. To do this, make your default browser Mozilla Firefox by following the steps mentioned in the preceding section.

Thereafter customize default search engine on Mozilla Firefox by following the instructions below:

1. Open the Menu tab
2. Go to **Options**

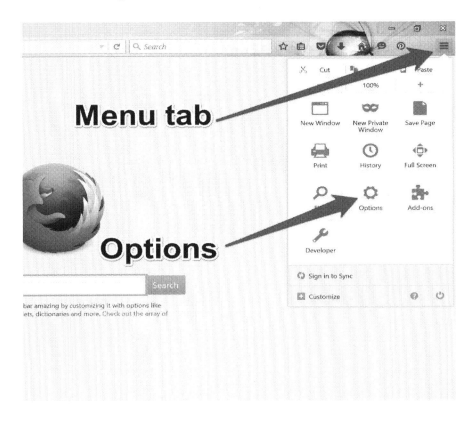

3. Then click on **Search** and then choose a default search engine from the list that appears.

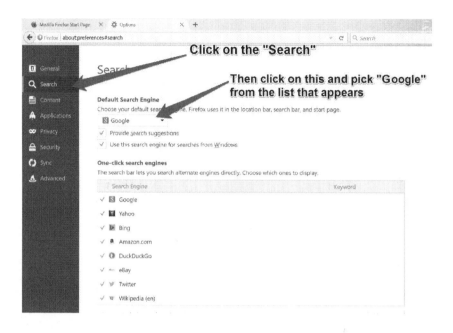

Please note that you may need a browser extension to for Cortana to use Google search engine if you are using Google Chrome as your default browser. You can get this extension by searching for **Bing2Google**.

Other things you may like to know about Cortana

One cool feature that not many people know about is the fact that you can completely hide the Cortana icon/panel. You may also reduce the Cortana search bar to just a small icon. To do this:

1. Right click on the Cortana's search box and then click on **Cortana**

2. Then choose any of the following:

- **Hidden:** Choose this option to completely hide this virtual assistant

- **Show Cortana icon:** Choose this option to reduce Cortana to a small icon on the taskbar

- **Show Search box:** Choose this option to display the Cortana search box. This is the default option.

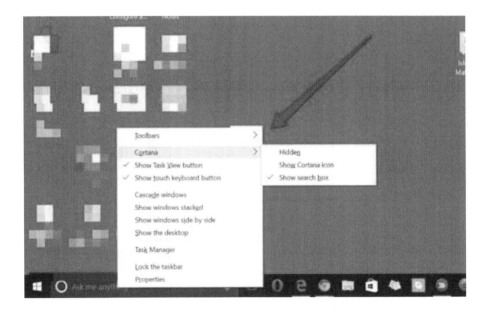

Troubleshooting Cortana

Although much efforts have been put into making this virtual assistant, I am quite sure that Cortana will misbehave at one time or the other. When this happen there are few things to do.

- **Ensure that you are connected to a strong network**: If you have bad or no internet connection, Cortana may not work properly. Therefore the first thing to check when Cortana starts to misbehave is the internet connection.

- **Use the keyboard**: You may need to use the keyboard to pass your message to Cortana if you find out that she is not getting your speech. Many of what you say (If not all) can also be typed into the Cortana's search bar.

- **Try training Cortana**: You can always train Cortana to understand you better. Please go to page 76 to learn how to get started.

- **Try to Restart Your PC**: If you find out that all what I have mentioned above does not work, you may try restarting your PC because it may be that it is your PC or device that is confused and not Cortana.

Conclusion

Cortana is like a learning machine and it is built to improve as time goes on. If you are having difficulty passing your message across to her, you may try typing some of your commands into the search box. I strongly believe you will know how to use her more as time goes on. Don't forget that Rome was not built a day.

MAIL APP

Introduction

Microsoft Surface Pro 4 and Microsoft Surface Book come preloaded with Mail app for sending and receiving emails and one of the things you will need to do when you start using your device is to set up an email account.

Your device Mail app has support for IMAP and POP accounts. In this section of the guide, you will be learning how to set up the Mail App and maximize it. So let's get started!

How to Add Your Email Accounts to Mail app

You probably have many email accounts and you may wish to add these accounts to the Mail app on your device.

Note: If you have already connected Microsoft account to the user account on your device, then Windows will automatically add your Microsoft account to the Mail app. However, you will still need follow the steps I am about to mention to add other email accounts to the Mail App.

The email accounts you can add to Mail app include Google Mail, Yahoo Mail, iCloud, Exchange, Outlook among others.

To add an email account:

- Click the **Start** button located at the lower left corner of the screen.

- On the Start menu, click on **Mail.**

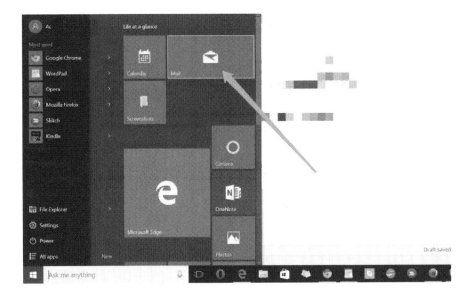

- If you are starting the Mail app for the first time, click on **Get Started.**

As shown below Windows has automatically added my Microsoft account to the Mail app. You can click on **Add account** button to add another account.

If you are not starting the Mail app for the first time and you wish to add another account, click **Settings** button and then click **Accounts** (as shown below).

Click **Add account** and then choose an account from the list that appears.

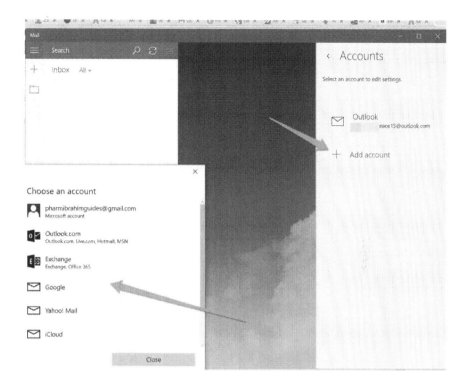

Fill in the details by typing in your email address and password and click on **Sign-in**

That is all! Mail adds your email account to the Mail Account.

Please note that you may be prompted to select what you want to share with Windows during the Mail app setup process, I will implore you to carefully go through all the items on the list before clicking **Allow.**

Special Note on Adding Exchange Account to Mail App

Following the instructions above might not be enough when you want to add your exchange account to Mail app and you may need extra information. You may need to obtain from your Exchange administrator or provider the account's server address, domain name, and username in addition to your email address and password.

How to Compose and Send an Email Message Using Mail App

You can easily send an email message to your friends or organization using the Mail App, in this section of the guide, we will be exploring how to compose an email message, how to save an email message as draft and how to send an email message. I will also take time to talk about how to format a text when composing an email message.

To send an email message:

- Tap on the plus (+) icon located on the Mail account pane.

- Type in the email address of the recipient

- To send a copy to another person, click on **Cc & Bcc** and type the person's email address in the **Cc** field.

- Type a subject for the message (The Subject section is immediately below the address section)

- You can use the **Format** tab to perform the following actions:

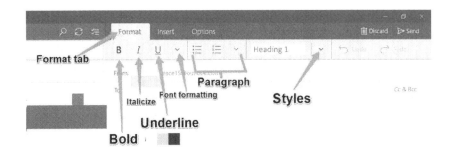

1. **Bold**: You can bold a part or your entire message using this feature. To bold a text, click the **B** icon.

2. **Italicize**: You can make your text appear italicized by clicking on the *I* icon.

3. **Underline**: Use the <u>U</u> icon to underline a text.

4. **Font formatting**: Use this option to add superscript/subscript to a text, change the font color of a text, strikethrough a text, change the font size or clear any formatting on a text.

5. **Paragraph**: Use this option to add special paragraphing features to your text just like you do with Microsoft Word. You can add bullet, Numbering, Special Indent, Space before Paragraph and Space after Paragraph using this option.

6. **Styles:** Use this tab to add headings, title, spacing, and quotes to your message.

Note: Before you can apply any of the formatting options above, you will need to select the text that you want to format. In addition, I will advise that you always use the formatting tab when composing an email; it makes your message easier to read.

- Use the **Insert** tab to perform the following:

- **Attachment**: You can insert an attachment into your message by clicking on **Attach**. This opens a dialog box. Locate and click on the file you want to attach and then click **Open** (located at the lower right corner of the dialog box).

- **Table**: Use this option to insert a table into your message. To insert a table, position your cursor to where you want the table to appear, and then click on the **Table.** Use the following options to customize your table:

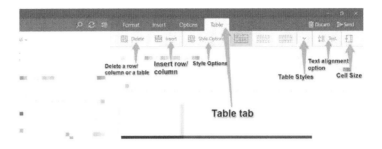

Table tab

- **Delete**: Use this option to delete a row, column, or the entire table.

- **Insert:** Use this option to insert more columns or rows to your table.

- **Style Options:** Use this option to add various styles to your table. Please note that the style you choose may not be obvious if the table style option does not support it.

- **Table Styles:** Use this option to customize how the table will look like. This option determines whether your table will be just a block of lines or something more elegant.

- **Text:** Use this option to choose how the text in your table will look like. You can use this option to align the text the way you like. Please note that you will need to select a text before you can align it.

- **Cell Size:** Use this option to choose how the individual cell in the table will look like. Use this option to adjust the width size of a row or column.

- **Picture:** You can also insert an image or logo into your message. To insert an image, position the cursor where you want the picture to appear, and click **Pictures.** This opens a dialog box, locate and click the picture you want to insert and then click **Insert.** To adjust the picture size or crop the picture, click the picture and click on **Crop.** If you want to restore the image to the way it was, click the image and then click on **Reset Size.** In addition, you can also rotate a picture by clicking on **Rotate.**

- **Link:** Use this option to add a link to your message.

- Use the **Options** tab to spell checks your message. You can also change the language selection for your message using this tab. In addition, use this tab to add level of importance to your message. You can choose between low importance and high importance.

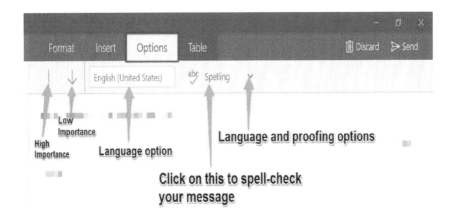

- When you are satisfied with the message and you are ready to send it, click on **Send** located the top right corner of the Mail app.

Saving a Message as a Draft

If you don't wish to send your message right away, you can save it as a draft. Mail app saves your message automatically as a draft; all you need to do is to click elsewhere in the Mail Window. For example, you may click the **Inbox** while composing a message to prompt the Mail app to save your composition as a draft.

You can locate the draft message by clicking on **Drafts** usually located below **Inbox.** To delete a draft, open the draft message and click on **Discard** (located beside **Send**).

Understanding the Different Folders in Mail App

There are many folders under individual accounts in Mail App, These folders are highlighted below:

Inbox: Contains messages sent to your email address.

Draft: Contains those messages you have started composing but you have not finished up with.

Sent: This holds copies of the messages you have sent at one time or the other.

Outbox: This holds outgoing messages that are in the process of being sent.

Junk: This is similar to spam box. This holds those messages that Mail has deemed to be unsolicited for. I will advise that you check you Junk email box before emptying it because Mail app may mistakenly classify a message as junk.

Thrash: This folder holds messages that you have deleted from other folders.

Mail App Keyboard Shortcuts

The following are the keyboard shortcut that you may need to use when using Mail app.

1. **Ctrl + B:** Bold

2. **Ctrl + U**: Underline

3. **Ctrl + I**: Italicize

4. **Ctrl + N**: New message

5. **Ctrl + Z**: Undo

6. **Ctrl + Y**: Redo

Managing a Received Email

One of the most important functions of any email app is ability to receive incoming messages. By default, Mail app searches for new messages and alert you when there is one.

New messages are either stored in Inbox or Junk folder and these are the two places to check if you are expecting an email.

To see if there is a new message, click on **Refresh** button located beside the Magnifying Lens icon at the upper part of the Mail app.

To read a message:

- Click on the subject of the message to open the message text in the preview pane.

- A bar appears beside messages that you have not yet read. See the picture below

- The attachment icon means that a message has an attachment.

- The Mail app allows you to perform the following options on a message in your inbox(see the red boxes):

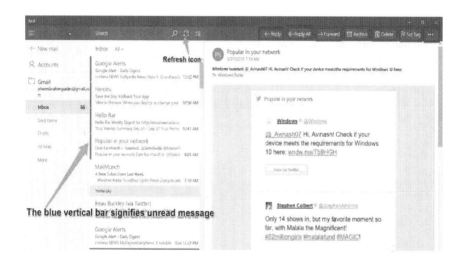

- **Reply:** Click this button to reply an email message. When you click this button, a new window appears. This window is similar to what appears when you click on **New mail** button but with a slight difference. This window already contains the recipient's name and the subject. In addition, the original message usually appears at the bottom of your reply for reference.

- **Reply All:** If the message in your inbox is addressed to several people, you can choose to reply all those people by clicking on **Reply All.** You can know whether an email is sent to many people by checking the email's **To** section.

- **Forward:** Use this option to send a copy of an email in your inbox to your friends or associates. When you click on the Forward button, a message windows with a subject line preceded by "FW:" appears. The original message's addresses (To and From), date, subject, attachment, and text are also included. In addition, you will have the option to fill in the email address of the person to whom you are sending the message. Use the **Cc & Bcc** to add other recipients (if any).

- **Delete:** Use this option to move the email to the trash bin.

- **Set Flag:** You can use this option to mark an email so that you may deal with it at a later time.

- **Three Dots (More) Icon:** Click on this icon to gain access to options like **Move** and **Print.** The **Move** option allows you to change the location of an email from one to another.

Hint: When you open the Mail app inbox to check a mail, the name of sender is usually displayed on the top of the message pane. To see the email address for whoever sent the message, click the name. If you are using a touch device, tap the name using your finger. A pop-box will show up displaying the email address.

How to Open and Save an Attachment in Mail App

The email with an attachment will have a paper clip icon displayed next to the address of the sender when you check your message inbox.

To open an attachment:

1. Click the message that has the attachment, as indicated by a paper clip.

2. When the message opens, click the attachment that you want to open.

3. The file then opens in the appropriate program. If your PC is not having an appropriate program to open the attachment, you may see a message like, "Windows can't open this type of file". In a situation like this, you will need to install the appropriate program for the type of file. You may ask the person that sent the message about which program to use to open the attachment.

To save an attachment:

1. Repeat the first step above. Then right click the attachment that you want to save and choose **Save.**

2. The **Save As** dialog box appears. Click the folder where you want to store the file. You can edit the name of attachment using the **File name** section.

3. Click **Save** when you are done.

How to Restore a Deleted Message

You may change your mind after deleting a message and may wish to restore it. To restore a deleted message:

1. Click **More** or **All folder** (located under the account name)

2. Click **Trash** or **Deleted Items**

3. Right click the message that you want to restore and select **Move.**

4. Click **Inbox.** You may also choose another folder if you like.

How to Create a Folder in Mail App

You may want to create a folder to get you email more organized. Creating a new folder helps you de-clutter your message inbox. By saving different emails to different folders, you make it easier to locate a message in the future.

Unfortunately, it appears that you may not be able to create a folder directly from the Mail app. You will need to create a folder using a web browser.

To create a folder:

1. Open mail.live.com from your web browser and sign in to your account.

2. Click **New Folder**

3. Type the name of the folder and press enter.

Please note that the new folder may not immediately appear in your Mail app, I will advise that you allow some minutes to pass.

To move a message to the newly created folder, right click the message and choose **Move,** then select the name of the folder from the list.

To rename your folder, sign-in into mail.live.com and right click the folder you want to rename. Then select **Rename** and enter a new name, press enter when you are done.

How to Change the Background of Mail App

You may want to select a different background image for the Mail app. To do this, open the Mail app, and click on the **Settings** icon (located at the left lower part of the app), then click **Background Picture.** Click on **Browse...** and choose an image from your library. Then click on **Open.**

Managing the Settings Options

Some of the options under Mail Settings have already been discussed. But let me briefly explain some of the options that have not been discussed.

Note: To access the Mail app settings, click on the settings icon located at the lower left corner of the app.

Reading: The options under this tab include:

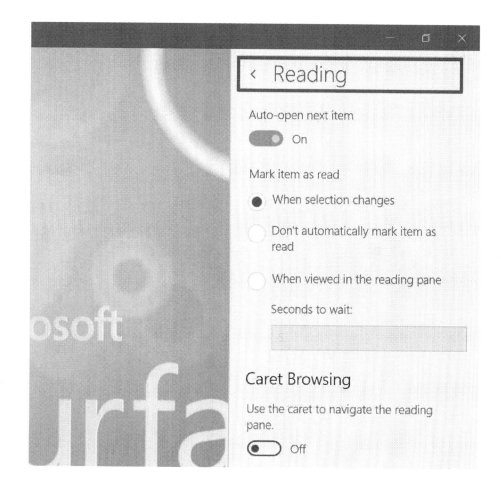

- **Auto-open next item:** When this option is **On,** Mail automatically opens the next message after you use swipe gesture to delete a message.

- **Mark item as read:** You can use this option to mark an item as read when you perform some certain actions like viewing an email in the reading pane.

- **Caret Browsing:** Use this option to tell Mail app to use the caret to navigate the reading pane or not. A **Caret** looks like this > or <

Options: The options under this tab include:

- **Swipe actions**: If you do not want to use a gesture on a tablet PC, select **Off** under this option.

- **Swipe right / hover:** Use this option to select what windows will do when you swipe right on a message.

- **Swipe left/hover:** Use this option to select what windows will do when you swipe left on a message.

- **Signature:** Use this option to tell Mail app what signature to include in a message. You can also edit signature message using this option. If you don't want to see any signature, select **Off** under this option.

Note: An email signature is a text that appears by default after the body of your message. You may set your email signature to be your name or your brand.

Other settings options are:

Help: Click this to get Microsoft help

Trust Center: Microsoft uses this option to give you locally relevant content

Feedback: Click this option if you like to give a feedback

About: Click this option to know more about the Mail app

How to Remove the Default Email Signature in Mail App

To remove an email signature in Mail app, please refer to page 107.

Conclusion

Mail App is a cool app and I will really love that you get the best out of it. Using this guide will not only get you started you started but it will also get you going with this app.

Thanks for reading my guide and I hope that this guide will get you started with these three top features on Microsoft Surface Pro 4 and Microsoft Surface Book.

Finally, if you will like to contact me on anything, please send me an email at **pharmibrahimguides@gmail.com**

Made in the USA
Middletown, DE
06 December 2015